SCHOLASTIC
News
Nonfiction Readers

Police Officers on the Go!

By Alyse Sweeney

Children's Press®
A Division of Scholastic Inc.
New York Toronto London Auckland Sydney
Mexico City New Delhi Hong Kong
Danbury, Connecticut

These content vocabulary word builders are for grades 1–2.
Subject Consultant: Brad Lucchini, Sergeant, Elmhurst Police Department, Elmhurst, Illinois

Reading Consultant: Cecilia Minden-Cupp, PhD, Former Director of the Language and Literacy Program, Harvard Graduate School of Education, Cambridge, Massachusetts

Photographs © 2007: AP/Wide World Photos: 20 bottom (George Nikitin), 21 top (Mike Virtanen); Corbis Images: 23 top left (Randy Faris), 4 bottom left, 15 (Fat Chance Productions), 13 (Tom Nebbia); Getty Images/Stockdisc Classic: 23 bottom right; Index Stock Imagery/Kevin Beebe: cover; JupiterImages/Comstock Images: 23 top right; PhotoEdit: 5 top left, 9, 11 (Spencer Grant), 20 top (James Shaffer), 5 top right, 10 (Dana White); ShutterStock, Inc./Johanna Goodyear: 2, 23 bottom left; Thaddeus Harden: back cover, 1, 4 bottom right, 4 top, 5 bottom right, 5 bottom left, 6, 7, 17, 18, 19, 21 bottom.

Book Design: Simonsays Design!
Book Production: The Design Lab

Library of Congress Cataloging-in-Publication Data

Sweeney, Alyse.
  Police officers on the go! / by Alyse Sweeney.
    p. cm. — (Scholastic news nonfiction readers)
  Includes bibliographical references and index.
  ISBN-10: 0-531-16810-7
  ISBN-13: 978-0-531-16810-3
  1. Police—Juvenile literature. I. Title. II. Series.
  HV7922.S94 2007
  363.2'3—dc22   2006015656

1 2 3 4 5 6 7 8 9 10 R 16 15 14 13 12 11 10 09 08 07

CONTENTS

Word Hunt 4-5

Proud to Be a Police Officer 6-7

The Dispatcher 8-9

The Police Lab 10-11

The Police Dog 12-13

How Officers Get Around 14-15

How Officers Talk to Each Other . . . 16-17

How Officers End Their Day 18-19

**There Are Many Different Kinds
of Police Officers** 20-21

Your New Words 22

**What Are Other Tools a Police
Officer Needs?** 23

Index 24

Meet the Author 24

WORD HUNT

Look for these words as you read. They will be in **bold**.

badge
(baj)

patrol car
(puh-**trohl** car)

police officers
(puh-**leess of**-uh-surz)

4

dispatcher
(diss-**pach**-er)

fingerprint
(**fing**-gur-print)

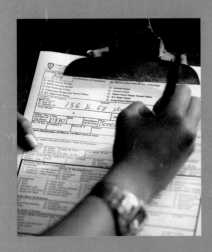

police report
(puh-**leess** ri-**port**)

two-way radio
(**too**-way
ray-dee-oh)

5

Proud to Be a Police Officer

Police officers keep people safe. They make sure people follow the laws.

Helping people makes police officers proud to wear their **badge**.

badge

Police officers start their day at the police station.

Many people work in a police station.

A **dispatcher** answers the phone when people dial the emergency number, 9-1-1.

The dispatcher tells the officers about the emergency and where they need to go.

A dispatcher answers emergency calls.

Some police officers work in the police lab.

The lab is where they look at clues, such as this **fingerprint**.

Clues help police officers solve crimes.

fingerprint

This police officer looks at fingerprints in the police lab.

This police dog is an important part of the police team, too!

Police dogs are great at helping officers find and rescue people.

How? With their super sense of smell!

This police officer and her dog work together to help people.

Police officers spend most of their time out in the community.

Some ride in a **patrol car**.

Others travel on bikes or motorcycles. A few officers even ride on horses.

Patrol cars help police officers to get where they need to go quickly.

"Come in, Officer Dave."

"Officer Dave here."

"There's an accident at 36 Burk Street."

"I'll be right there."

A **two-way radio** helps officers talk to the dispatcher and to each other.

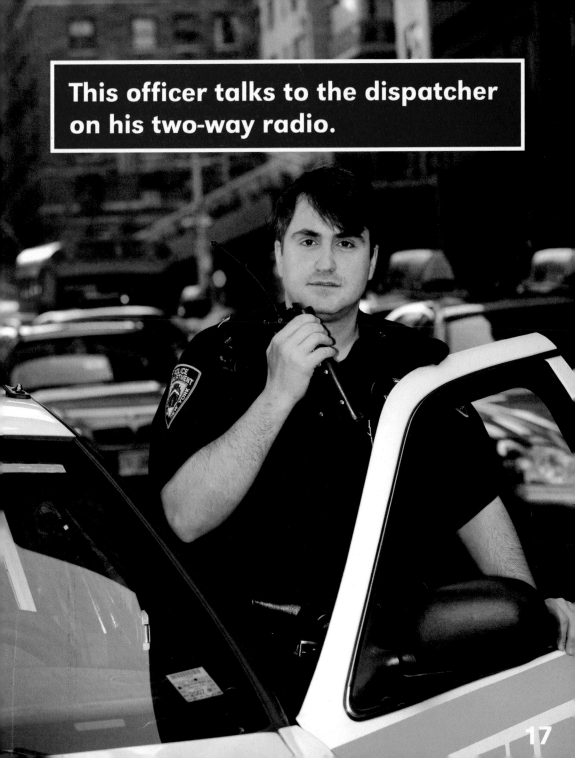

This officer talks to the dispatcher on his two-way radio.

At the end of the day, police officers fill out a **police report**. The report describes what happened that day.

Police officers are always ready to help and protect the community!

police report

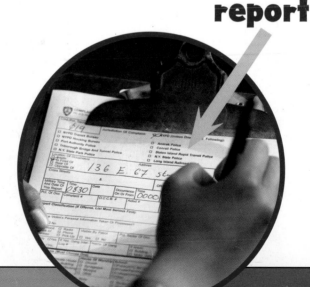

THERE ARE MANY DIFFERENT KINDS OF POLICE OFFICERS

Detectives are police officers who help solve crimes by looking for clues. They do not wear a uniform.

Fish and game wardens protect fish and animals that live in the wild. They also make sure that people follow fishing, hunting, and boating laws.

Forest rangers protect forests and help stop forest fires. These forest rangers also help keep people safe when they camp or hike in the forest.

Harbor police protect harbors. They help injured animals and fight fires on boats and docks.

YOUR NEW WORDS

badge (baj) a small sign that is worn on clothing or a uniform

dispatcher (diss-**pach**-er) a person who answers emergency calls

fingerprint (**fing**-gur-print) a mark made when a fingertip is pressed in ink and then pressed onto paper

patrol car (puh-**trohl** car) a car that a police officer drives

police officers (puh-**leess of**-uh-surz) people who keep others safe and make sure that laws are followed

police report (puh-**leess** ri-**port**) a description of what a police officer does each day

two-way radio (**too-way ray**-dee-oh) a tool that lets police officers talk to each other

WHAT ARE OTHER TOOLS A POLICE OFFICER NEEDS?

flashing lights

flashlight

handcuffs

loudspeaker

23

INDEX

badges, 6
bikes, 14

clues, 10, 20
crimes, 10, 20

detectives, 20
dispatchers, 8, 16

emergency number
    (9-1-1), 8

fingerprints, 10
fires, 21
fish and game wardens,
    20
forest rangers, 21

harbor police, 21
horses, 14

laws, 6, 20

motorcycles, 14

patrol cars, 14
police dogs, 12
police labs, 10
police reports, 18
police stations, 8

two-way radios, 16

FIND OUT MORE

Book:
Liebman, Daniel. *I Want to Be a Police Officer*. Toronto: Firefly Books, 2000.

Web site:
Midvale Police Kids Page
http://www.midvalepolice.org/kids.htm

MEET THE AUTHOR:

Alyse Sweeney is a freelance writer who has published more than twenty books and poems for children. Prior to becoming a freelance writer, she was a teacher, reading specialist, and Scholastic editor. Alyse lives in Las Vegas, Nevada, with her husband and two children.